FRANCIS FRITH'S

PETERSFIELD
THEN AND NOW

PHOTOGRAPHIC MEMORIES

KENNETH HICK is an engineer who became a Member of the Institute of Public Relations through a career change with his company into public and media relations. Kenneth's first memory of Petersfield is the destruction by fire of Norman Burton's shop in 1948. He has been town mayor three times, first beoming a local councillor in the town in 1965. Kenneth loves Petersfield and the values that it stands for and strives to give back everything that living in the town has given him. Interests of travel and singing have combined to take him to Germany, Finland, Italy, the USA, Malta, Jersey etc.

FRANCIS FRITH'S
PHOTOGRAPHIC MEMORIES

PETERSFIELD
THEN AND NOW

PHOTOGRAPHIC MEMORIES

KENNETH HICK

First published in the United Kingdom in 2004 by
Frith Book Company Ltd

Limited Hardback Subscribers Edition Published in 2004
ISBN 1-85937-861-7

Paperback Edition 2004
ISBN 1-85937-862-5

British Library Cataloguing in Publication Data

Francis Frith's Petersfield Then And Now - Photographic
Memories
Kenneth Hick

Frith Book Company Ltd
Frith's Barn, Teffont,
Salisbury, Wiltshire SP3 5QP
Tel: +44 (0) 1722 716 376
Email: info@francisfrith.co.uk
www.francisfrith.co.uk

Printed and bound in Great Britain

Front Cover: **PETERSFIELD**, *High Street* P48010
Frontispiece: **PETERSFIELD**, *The Railway Restaurant and the
Wesleyan Church 1906* 54416

*The colour-tinting is for illustrative purposes only, and is not intended to be his-
torically accurate*

2004 images supplied by Kenneth Hick

AS WITH ANY HISTORICAL DATABASE THE FRITH ARCHIVE IS CONSTANTLY
BEING CORRECTED AND IMPROVED AND THE PUBLISHERS WOULD WELCOME
INFORMATION ON OMISSIONS OR INACCURACIES

CONTENTS

FRANCIS FRITH: VICTORIAN PIONEER   *7*

PETERSFIELD THEN AND NOW - AN INTRODUCTION   *10*

BURITON   *14*

EAST MEON   *18*

FROXFIELD   *24*

LISS   *28*

THE MARKET PLACE   *38*

SHOPPING STREETS   *46*

SHEET AND STEEP   *76*

WEST MEON AND HARTING   *84*

INDEX   *89*

NAMES OF SUBSCRIBERS   *90*

Free Mounted Print Voucher   *93*

I wish to acknowledge the help and encouragement extended to me by people who in all honesty know more about the town than I do. In particular I single out Mary Ray, Roy Kersley and Pat White from Liss. I would wish to acknowledge the help given to me by Jean, my wife, who also was good enough to proof read my text for me.

Over the years many of the town's inhabitants have kindled my interest in my home town. To mention but a few, Bert Ifould, Peter Marshall and the late Leslie Nation. Most of all I wish to record the contribution of the late Gilbert Hobbs, who was most knowledgeable about the town's past and whose friendship engendered in me the need to distinguish fact from fiction in order to arrive at the realities of the history of Petersfield

FRANCIS FRITH
VICTORIAN PIONEER

FRANCIS FRITH, founder of the world-famous photographic archive, was a complex and multi-talented man. A devout Quaker and a highly successful Victorian businessman, he was philosophical by nature and pioneering in outlook.

By 1855 he had already established a wholesale grocery business in Liverpool, and sold it for the astonishing sum of £200,000, which is the equivalent today of over £15,000,000. Now a very rich man, he was able to indulge his passion for travel. As a child he had pored over travel books written by early explorers, and his fancy and imagination had been stirred by family holidays to the sublime mountain regions of Wales and Scotland. 'What lands of spirit-stirring and enriching scenes and places!' he had written. He was to return to these scenes of grandeur in later years to 'recapture the thousands of vivid and tender memories', but with a different purpose. Now in his thirties, and captivated by the new science of photography, Frith set out on a series of pioneering journeys up the Nile and to the

Near East that occupied him from 1856 until 1860.

INTRIGUE AND EXPLORATION

These far-flung journeys were packed with intrigue and adventure. In his life story, written when he was sixty-three, Frith tells of being held captive by bandits, and of fighting 'an awful midnight battle to the very point of surrender with a deadly pack of hungry, wild dogs'. Wearing flowing Arab costume, Frith arrived at Akaba by camel sixty years before Lawrence of Arabia, where he encountered 'desert princes and rival sheikhs, blazing with jewel-hilted swords'.

He was the first photographer to venture beyond the sixth cataract of the Nile. Africa was still the mysterious 'Dark Continent', and Stanley and Livingstone's historic meeting was a decade into the future. The conditions for picture taking confound belief. He laboured for hours in his wicker dark-room in the sweltering heat of the desert, while the volatile chemicals fizzed dangerously in their trays. Back in London he exhibited his photographs and was 'rapturously cheered' by members of the Royal Society. His reputation as a photographer was made overnight.

VENTURE OF A LIFE-TIME

Characteristically, Frith quickly spotted the opportunity to create a new business as a specialist publisher of photographs. He lived in an era of immense and sometimes violent change.

For the poor in the early part of Victoria's reign work was exhausting and the hours long, and people had precious little free time to enjoy themselves. Most had no transport other than a cart or gig at their disposal, and rarely travelled far beyond the boundaries of their own town or village. However, by the 1870s the railways had threaded their way across the country, and Bank Holidays and half-day Saturdays had been made obligatory by Act of Parliament. All of a sudden the working man and his family were able to enjoy days out and see a little more of the world.

With typical business acumen, Francis Frith foresaw that these new tourists would enjoy having souvenirs to commemorate their days out. In 1860 he married Mary Ann Rosling and set out on a new career: his aim was to photograph every city, town and village in Britain. For the next thirty years he travelled the country by train and by pony and trap, producing fine photographs of seaside resorts and beauty spots that were keenly bought by millions of Victorians. These prints were painstakingly pasted into family albums and pored over during the dark nights of winter, rekindling precious memories of summer excursions.

THE RISE OF FRITH & CO

Frith's studio was soon supplying retail shops all over the country. To meet the demand he gathered about him a small team of photographers, and published the work of independent artist-photographers of the calibre of Roger Fenton and Francis Bedford. In order to gain some understanding of the scale of Frith's business one only has to look at the catalogue issued by Frith & Co in 1886: it runs to some 670 pages, listing not only many thousands of views of the British Isles but also many photographs of most European countries, and China, Japan, the USA and Canada - note the sample page shown on page 9 from the hand-written Frith & Co ledgers recording the pictures. By 1890 Frith had created the greatest specialist photographic publishing company in the world, with over 2,000 sales outlets - more than the combined number that Boots and WH Smith have today! The picture on the next page shows the Frith & Co display board at Ingleton in the Yorkshire Dales (left of window). Beautifully constructed with a mahogany frame and gilt inserts, it could display up to a dozen local scenes.

POSTCARD BONANZA

The ever-popular holiday postcard we know today took many years to develop. In 1870 the Post Office issued the first plain cards, with a pre-printed stamp on one face. In 1894 they allowed other publishers' cards to be sent through the mail with an attached adhesive halfpenny stamp. Demand grew rapidly, and in 1895 a new size of postcard was permitted called the court card, but there was little room for illustration. In 1899, a year after Frith's death, a new card measuring 5.5 x 3.5 inches became the standard format, but it was not until 1902 that the divided back came into being, so that the address and message could be on one face and a full-size illustration on the other. Frith & Co were in the vanguard of postcard development: Frith's sons Eustace and Cyril continued their father's monumental task, expanding the number of views offered to the public and recording more and more places in Britain, as the

5		
6	St Catherine's College	+
7	Senate House & Library	+
8		+
9	Gerrard Hostel Bridge	+ + + +
3 0	Geological Museum	
1	Addenbrooke's Hospital	+
2	St Mary's Church	+
3	Fitzwilliam Museum, Pitt Press &c	+
4		+
5	Buxton, The Crescent	+
6	The Colonnade	+
7	Public Gardens	+
8		+
9	Haddon Hall, View from the Terrace	+
4 0	Miller's Dale	+

coasts and countryside were opened up to mass travel.

Francis Frith had died in 1898 at his villa in Cannes, his great project still growing. The archive he created continued in business for another seventy years. By 1970 it contained over a third of a million pictures showing 7,000 British towns and villages.

FRANCIS FRITH'S LEGACY

Frith's legacy to us today is of immense significance and value, for the magnificent archive of evocative photographs he created provides a unique record of change in the cities, towns and villages throughout Britain over a century and more. Frith and his fellow studio photographers revisited locations many times down the years to update their views, compiling for us an enthralling and colourful pageant of British life and character.

We are fortunate that Frith was dedicated to recording the minutiae of everyday life. For it is this sheer wealth of visual data, the painstaking chronicle of changes in dress, transport, street layouts, buildings, housing, engineering and landscape that captivates us so much today. His remarkable images offer us a powerful link with the past and with the lives of our ancestors.

THE VALUE OF THE ARCHIVE TODAY

Computers have now made it possible for Frith's many thousands of images to be accessed almost instantly. Frith's images are increasingly used as visual resources, by social historians, by researchers into genealogy and ancestry, by architects and town planners, and by teachers involved in local history projects.

In addition, the archive offers every one of us an opportunity to examine the places where we and our families have lived and worked down the years. Highly successful in Frith's own era, the archive is now, a century and more on, entering a new phase of popularity. Historians consider the Francis Frith Collection to be of prime national importance. It is the only archive of its kind remaining in private ownership. Francis Frith's archive is now housed in an historic timber barn in the beautiful village of Teffont in Wiltshire. Its founder would not recognize the archive office as it is today. In place of the many thousands of dusty boxes containing glass plate negatives and an all-pervading odour of photographic chemicals, there are now ranks of computer screens. He would be amazed to watch his images travelling round the world at unimaginable speeds through internet lines.

The archive's future is both bright and exciting. Francis Frith, with his unshakeable belief in making photographs available to the greatest number of people, would undoubtedly approve of what is being done today with his lifetime's work. His photographs depicting our shared past are now bringing pleasure and enlightenment to millions around the world a century and more after his death.

PETERSFIELD THEN AND NOW
AN INTRODUCTION

WE DO NOT HAVE to guess when Petersfield was born, we know! It was very close to 1120 AD. You will not find mention of the town in the Domesday Book because it did not exist at that time. Petersfield was a new town, laid out in response to the increased prosperity that followed the Norman Conquest, and the ability of landowners to enhance their income by establishing towns as centres of trade.

Although the original charter, granted by Earl William of Gloucester, grandson of King Henry I, has been lost, Hawissa, widow of Earl William, confirmed the charter of her late husband in 1183.

'Know all men present and to come that I, Hawissa, Countess of Gloucester have granted and confirm to my Burgesses of Petersfield who have built and are settled, and who shall build in it, all liberties and free customs in the same Borough which the citizens of Winchester have in their city.'

All was written on a parchment no larger than a piece of today's A5 paper.

It is possible that the town grew up around the Market Place, which could have been at a crossroads between the road that wound its way up from the coast at Portsmouth into The Spain as we know it, and the west to east route which can be traced from Winchester and The Stroud across to Durford Abbey and into the dark woods of Sussex. The Spain could well have been an extension or ancillary space to the market.

But there may be a flaw to this theory. The question must be posed, why did prehistoric man find the area so attractive that he built at least 21 barrows around what we now call the Heath? It suggests a high population in the area over a long period of time. There are also the remains of a Roman villa at The Stroud to consider; as they are just a short way from the east - west route through the town there must have been some attraction to the owner to build on that spot.

As it is, the positioning of the new town is important. The Square and the High Street are strategically placed between the two streams that flow to the east away from habitation. They bring fresh water supplies from the springs that issue below the escarpment which dominates to the west. The land runs away down Sheep Street and Dragon Street to the south stream and down Ramswalk and Chapel Street to the north stream. This would provide the town centre with adequate water for its needs.

It is easy to imagine a chapel of rest on the site of St Peter's Church which would serve the needs of worshippers who were working in the fields away from their homes in Buriton. So we have the name of Petersfield! As with so many churches it would have been built on the highest point so that it could be seen from all around, and have been close to the speculative crossroads.

The downs around the town were ideal lands for grazing sheep and would have been a source of immense trade. Mutton greatly appealed to the Norman palate and the development of improved weaving techniques and the town's somewhat damp atmosphere created a natural centre for the woollen cloth (Kersey) industry in the town. Fulling or pounding mills required only a modest head of water to operate and this would be within the capabilities of both the north and south streams. These mills not only washed the fleeces but, with the help of fuller's earth, also removed much of the lanolin grease from the wool.

The lower land gave excellent pasture for dairy herds and together the hides of sheep and cows provided the raw materials for a leather industry. This appears to have been based around the south stream in the area now occupied by Hylton Road and the Tesco store. It would not have been sited further upstream as the waste from the processes would have been foul, to say the least, and the smell would have stifled the town itself.

Petersfield is geologically a complex town with outcrops of clay and sand; to the south and west there is chalk in abundance. Where water meets impervious layers of clay, it runs over the top of the clay and emerges in springs which are all around the town and often create little marshy areas. The clay was exploited in a tile industry; indeed when looking for the derivation of the

PETERSFIELD, *The High Street c1955* P48010

name 'The Spain', one reasonable explanation is that, instead of thatch, the houses in The Spain were roofed with the superior 'spaynes' or tiles.

Towards the south, clay predominates from halfway up the Causeway and it was here that the last brickworks were situated immediately to the north of the Jolly Sailor. Come to the north of the town and there are the remains of sandpits at the community centre, at the far end of Madeline Road, behind Penns Road and what is now the Borough Road recreation ground. Together with the lime, produced from chalk and used in mortar, the town had all the elements for building the replacements for time-ravaged mediaeval buildings in the Georgian era.

The Portsmouth - London road replaced the wool industry as the important factor in the town's economy and from 1600 onwards the 'inn' trade developed. Petersfield became famous for its hostelries both within the High Street and, with the coming of the turnpike (1721), along what are now College and Dragon Streets (the Red Lion, the Green Dragon, the Dolphin etc.) Within a half day's journey of Portsmouth, the home of the British Navy, Petersfield's coaching inns reached their zenith during the years between the Napoleonic wars and the coming of the railway in 1858/9.

The railway brought increased prosperity to the town and with it, yet another building boom. Lavant Street connected Chapel Street to the new railway station bringing commerce to Chapel Street and substantial Victorian properties to Lavant Street. This then became the place to be for the new well-to-do. Substantial properties were also built on the eastern end of Station Road and along the new road skirting the north-west boundary of the The Heath. Although these were large houses in today's terms, their owners did not 'keep their carriages'.

In the aftermath of World War I, manufacturing industry found Petersfield to be fertile ground; its communications with Portsmouth, London, and to the east and west along the A272 road, gave the town a great economic advantage. Petersfield's electricity had been generated at the local power station in Sandringham Road and when the town was connected to the infant national grid, the abandoned premises were taken over by the Levy brothers (1919-1987). Here they undertook the manufacture of ITS concave/convex rubber heels for boots and shoes. Their contribution to the World War II effort was the design and production of the famous 'Commando' cleated rubber soles for boots. Incidentally they also designed and made Minibrix the forerunner of the famous children's construction toy, Lego.

The other major manufacturing company operating in the town was Flextella Fencing and Engineering Company. The firm had its origins in two pre World War I factory units built between Frenchmans Road and the station; its well-known invention was chain link fencing. In 1946 its parent organisation, Portsmouth Steel, was taken over by the engineering company of J B Corrie.

The town's Festival Hall was opened 6 October 1935 and since then has contributed so much to the nature of Petersfield. In World War II it was the focus of fund raising for the war effort and was an important dance venue for a wide catchment - a function which carried on well into the sixties. By that time it had become a major East Hampshire centre for amateur performing arts, with three musical and two dramatic societies. These groups have forged a reputation for the town's artistic life which stretches far beyond its surrounding area. The Festival Hall is one of the South's best multipurpose halls. The Hall commemorates the renowned Petersfield Musical Festival which was, in 1935, responsible for its construction. The Musical Festival is still going strong after 100 years!

Always a centre for the surrounding agricultural area, Petersfield has been a continuous focus for local government but has lost its importance as a centre for law and order. At one time a divisional office for the Hampshire and Isle of Wight Constabulary, the police station now only opens at restricted times and the next-door magistrates court (1897) heard its last case 31 March 1995. The courthouse now provides an excellent museum of the heritage of the town and its surrounding area; it is a private museum and is run by the townsfolk.

Saying that you live in Petersfield is to invite the question, 'What did King William III have to do with Petersfield?' Nothing really, is the standard reply, William Joliffe left £500 in his will for the purchase and erection of the equestrian statue in New Way or as it is now called, St Peters Road. The statue is closely based on the magnificent Roman bronze statue of Marcus Aurelius in the Piazza del Campidoglio in Rome and was placed in its present position in The Square in 1812. This horse sired similar others in Paris, Dublin, Glasgow, London and Bristol. The purpose of those statues of William III was to perpetuate the memory of an upholder of the protestant cause in a post-Jacobean Great Britain.

Since the beginning of the 20th century, the town's population has risen from around 3,000 to nearly 14,000 today. It was praised as being the second-best place to live in the country during 1998 and has tried hard to maintain that position ever since. The balance between commerce and community, together with its position in the East Hampshire Area of Outstanding Natural Beauty, gives every reason for its people to live in harmony with one another.

PETERSFIELD, *Dragon Street c1965* P48046

BURITON

THIS ANCIENT VILLAGE features in the Domesday Book as Mapledrensham. It nestles close under the lee of the steep north face of the downs, as shelter from the effects of the weather on early buildings was important and the presence of a stream had an influence on its position. St Marys Church was, until 1886, the mother church of Petersfield. Buriton is home to a lively population with a vigorous community spirit.

For many years it was the goal for walkers on the South Downs Way, who had committed themselves to a journey from Eastbourne some 80 miles to the west across beautiful downland; now that goal has been carried further west along the Hampshire Downs to Winchester.

BURITON
The Vicarage 1898 41371

Over 100 years have passed since this photograph was taken. The view has survived the two world wars that changed our way of life forever. Could it be that the lack of change in this view brings with it all that we desire in village life? Even the sluice along the wall to the pond is still the same.

15

BURITON
The Vicarage 2004
B248701

A lot of ducks have
swum in the pond since
the previous photograph
but apart from a
signpost, nothing of
importance has
changed. Surely those
posts around the pond
are the same ones? By
the way, the Vicarage is
now known as the Old
Rectory.

BURITON, *The High Street 1898* 41373

Before the days of a piped water supply, the well to the left would be the focus of a village life well known to the little boy
standing at the doorway just beyond it. The chapel to the right is no more.

BURITON
The Manor House
c1960 B248007

The Manor House's most famous inhabitant was Edward Gibbon, who researched much of his book *The Decline and Fall of the Roman Empire* in this house. It is obvious that the original house is on the left with stately additions to the right. Another even older house forms the back of the impressive building.

BURITON, *The High Street 2004* B248702

The front of the chapel has been redeveloped; it now stands back from the road and provides pleasant housing. As to the rest of the photograph, the cottages are now one dwelling but even the boundary walls have changed little in over a century.

EAST MEON

A WALK around this village is most rewarding; very little imagination is needed to realize that you are in a very ancient landscape, which bears witness to all the factors influencing country life over the centuries. If you are ever in Bayeux visiting the displayed tapestry, you will find a fine model of this village as it was at the time of the Domesday Book! It is well worth visiting East Meon when the village gardens are open during the spring and summer. There may even be the possibility of visiting the historic 13th-century Court House, which is something to behold.

EAST MEON
The Village c1955 E173003

In fifty years, increased prosperity has ensured the preservation of these old buildings showing the quintessential English village. The effect is completed by the stream seen just to the left of the vanishing roadway.

19

► **EAST MEON**
The Village c1955
E173008

An infant River Meon heads off on its way to the sea at Titchfield Haven, with the High Street on both sides, while the women appear intent on something worth looking at in Mr Brooks' grocery shop window.

◄**EAST MEON**
The Village 2004
E173701

One would be hard pressed to spot any difference in this view which is almost identical to the one from 49 years ago. This view of the Cross is taken from the road going to West Meon. In fifty years this road has seen traffic increase tenfold (making the taking of this photograph somewhat hazardous).

▲ **EAST MEON,** *The Village 2004* E173702

Mr Brooks' grocery shop has been gone for many years now. The River Meon still threads its way through this delightful village to the sea. Just at the rear of this photograph is the end view of the new village shop and post office, the only change to the scene.

◄**EAST MEON**
Church Street c1965
E173012

Looking north to the church a sense of nostalgia is created by the old style 'T' junction road sign. Every spring the churchyard is full of golden daffodils, bringing visitors from far and near. The Ye Old George Inn sign depicting St George slaying the dragon, would do credit to any ancient town in Austria or Germany. Opposite is C P Smith's post office stores.

EAST MEON
Church Street 2004
E173703

The keen eye will spot the growth of the trees on the skyline, the absence of the road sign and a new chimmney stack just above the inn sign. The post office stores have moved around the corner and the letter box has gone.

FROXFIELD

BEST DESCRIBED as an area populated by farms, Froxfield does not possess a defined centre. Froxfield Green with its church is the heart of this village. For many years the Slade was the home of Roger Powell whose knowledge of the craft of bookbinding and restoration was second to none. He was called to Florence in 1966 to help with the restoration of priceless Renaissance treasures damaged by the disastrous flooding of Arno river.

FROXFIELD GREEN
The Stores and Post Office c1960 F188003

H C Cobb is the name above the shop, with beautifully designed windows which feature very thin styles. These had to be made from the best quality wood and allow the maximum light into the shop. The classic phone box displays the king's crown at the top centre of each pediment.

FROXFIELD GREEN
*The Old Stores and
Post Office 2004*
F188701

Time has certainly
wrought changes to the
fortunes of this building.
I wonder if Mr Cobb ever
thought that his post
office would end up
making such a delightful
house as this. What a
pity about the lovely
shop windows.

FROXFIELD GREEN, *A Thatched Cottage c1960* F188016

The cottage's window frames pay homage to the cast iron that came with the British industrial revolution. Although little changed from this 1960s view, there has since been an alteration to the right-hand chimney bringing it out to the end wall.

FROXFIELD GREEN, *The Lych Gate and War Memorial c1965* F188020

This wonderfully constructed lych gate looks as if it will last for ever. It is oak built and stands in the shade of an ancient yew tree. An inscription on the memorial says 'Sons of this place let this of you be said that you who live are worthy of your dead.' Sadly the village pump, to the left of the lych gate is no longer there.

LISS

If you are looking for Liss before 1859 you must visit what is now called West Liss where the old shops can still be found, some of them hiding behind the facades of domestic premises, others still in use as antique shops or offices. The Plestor Oak still stands in front of the Spread Eagle, which was also the site of the village stocks, and on the corner of Church Street is Liss's oldest building. St Peter's Church became too small to meet the needs of the new village which resulted from the building of the railway. It was also remote. Now the village has spread towards the railway and beyond.

LISS
Station Road 1901 46610

Every building in this photograph was built in the latter part of the reign of Queen Victoria, as the railway station of 1858/9 brought about the establishment of the village of Liss, sometimes called East Liss. At the end of the road you can see the signal box on the far side of the railway, beyond the Station Hotel, now the Crossing Gates pub. To the left, Mark Mitchell confirms his claim as poulterer judging by the chickens hanging outside his shop and the cart loaded with baskets and hampers waiting outside. On the right, a triangular sign indicates Temperance Restaurant and in the foreground, Paris
the 'cash grocer' also has a good selection of clothes in his window.

▼ **LISS,** *Station Road 2004* L54701

Now Mark Mitchell has a new shop nearer to us but the old one is still there, painted white and with the addition of an end gable in the roof. The signal box has gone and Mr Parish has given way to an Estate Agent.

▶ **LISS**

A Cottage 1901 46614

I have no clue as to where this cottage is nor can I find out anything about it. Can a kind reader help on this photograph? It looks like a washday Monday.

◄**WEST LISS**
*St Peter's Church
1901* 46616

The arrival of the railway one mile away, sealed the fate of West Liss. A new village was born around the railway station and with it a new church, St Mary's, built in 1892 by Sir Arthur Blomfield. Over the years this new church has led to the gradual demise of St Peter's, West Liss. Its future is now unsure.

► **LISS**
Station Road 1934
86045

Only small changes in 70 years, the Railway Hotel at the far end of the street is now the Whistle Stop. Advertisements for Carter's Seeds give a clue to the shop on the immediate left, it was the Southern Counties Agricultural Trading Society (SCATS). W E Allen was the chemist and next door, F C Rump sold cigarettes and picture postcards. At the far end of the street on the left is Noakes hardware shop.

LISS, *War Memorial Corner c1955* L54002

The names above the shops are recognised throughout the area as old Liss names - the name Langrish also appears on the memorial for World War I as one of those who gave their lives for their country. One of the shops has a picture of Noah's Ark on its gable end; the shop was built by Noah Carpenter.

LISS, *War Memorial Corner 2004* L54702

There have been recent alterations to this junction between Rake and Station Roads. The War Memorial has been moved away from the junction and there is a Chinese restaurant with a yellow awning next door to a one-hour photographic shop.

► **LISS**
Palmers, Rake Road
1934 86052

Probably one of the oldest houses in Liss, its origins go back to the days when pilgrims would stop at such houses along the way from Winchester to Canterbury. A cloister leads to the house from a point just to the right of the gateway. When this photograph was taken Palmers was owned by Herbert Newman Collard, a fruit grower and village beneficiary.

◀ **LISS**
Palmers, Rake Road
2004 L54703

In this contemporary
photograph, Tom Collard,
son of Herbert Newman
Collard, has just driven out of
the gate arch in the original
lovingly restored model 'T'
Ford bought by his father in
1916. Otherwise little if any
change.

PETERSFIELD
From Tilmore 1906
54393

A view across the town taken from above the Tilmore railway bridge. The Italianate dome to the right, is that of the then 16-year-old St Laurence's Roman Catholic Church and the spire to the left is that of the 3-year-old Wesleyan Methodist Church. In the centre but more distant, the 900-year-old St Peter's can be seen. The lady on the bridge would very likely be going to the shops - she is just about to pass over the second arch of the railway bridge which accommodated the branch line forking off to Midhurst (1864). Just below this view was the site of 'Benzo' Kimber's menagerie.

THE MARKET PLACE

NOW CALLED the Square, this is the natural centre of Petersfield life and has been over the centuries. Markets are held on Wednesdays and Saturdays and recently farmers' markets have come to town on the first Sunday of every month, bringing people from far and wide to the town. The Square has all the ingredients for harmony both of purpose and style. It has a Norman church, a library (1982), a psuedo-Georgian post office (1922) a stylish Co-op building (1954) and a twice-preserved Georgian front to the left of Ramswalk. One feature that is tucked away, is the original hurdle house, later to become gentlemen's toilets. This incorporates the arches from the Old Town Hall and used to be surmounted by the stone balls removed from the coping stones of Pince's School. Both were demolished in 1898. The last cattle were sold in the market on 12 December 1962.

PETERSFIELD
The Market Place 1898 41314

What a gem this photograph is. Prior to this, the Old Town Hall (1780), the offices of *The Hampshire Post* and Pince's School obscured the view of St Peter's from the Square. In 1898 these buildings were pulled down. This photograph was taken during this demolition because Pince's School still stands, but all that remains of the other two buildings is the pile of rubble on the left. The drinking fountain, centre middle distance, was about to begin its travels, first to a position in front of the church, then in 1977 to a pedestrian bridge over the stream near the present Ramswalk and, at the time of writing, at the eastern end of the central car park. Castle House stands behind the iron railings on the right, beside the George Inn.

39

▼ **PETERSFIELD,** *The Market Place 2004* P48701

The 1922 post office has taken the place of Castle House which went in 1913 and if you look you will see that the post office building line exactly corresponds to the line of Castle House boundary wall. One further difference is the heightened roof line of the small building next to the flat-roofed, three-storied building in front of the church tower.

▶ **PETERSFIELD**
The Market Place 1898
41315

Next to the George Inn (left) stands the late lamented Castle House (1597-1913), on a site now occupied by the post office and HSBC Bank. The hurdles and Sussex gates appear to be part of preparations for the immolation of William III, but actually they are to be used for the awaited cattle market.

40

PETERSFIELD
The Market Place
c1950 P48007

Move on 52 years from the last photograph, turn right-angles to your right, and the stalls are still the same but the car is making its presence felt. Behind the statue is the Forrest Stores, to its right SPQR Tobacconist's, Lee Bros. Hairdressers and Edward Privett, Gents Outfitters. Behind Ken Pett's green post office van on the left of the picture, you can just see the remains of Norman Burton's shop which burnt down during the early hours of 6 January 1948.

PETERSFIELD
The Market Place
c1950 P48009

This Wednesday morning 9 o'clock photograph is the first view we have in this book of Sheep Street in the far corner of the Square. The solitary cow tied to the railings gives a symbolic forewarning of the end of the cattle market some 12 years later. You could get your feet wet stepping down into the Southdown Omnibus Office over on the far side of the Square and what on earth is that greenhouse doing in front of the statue?

41

PETERSFIELD
The Market Place
c1955 P48039

In front of the George Inn is parked an Austin A90 Atlantic and next door is the post office with the apparatus and switchboard floors of the telephone exchange above. The Southdown 'Bus Office, together with Muriel Roberts, has moved across the Square to share the new building on the right which replaced the shop of Norman Burton.

PETERSFIELD, *The Square c1965* P48061

At the top centre of this view is No.1 the Square, the oldest building in the town. There is a gap in the stalls behind the statue where 'Fishy Arnett' presided over his stall, selling fish from the goodness of his heart, but never by weight! The entrance to the post office has moved one window to the left.

▲ **PETERSFIELD**
The Market Square c1965 P48068

The cattle trough on the far side of the Square in 1965 was about to vacate its position to one outside the offices slightly behind the telephone kiosk, where it has become a feature of 'Petersfield in Bloom'. The telephone box on the left is the famed leaning kiosk of Petersfield where it stands on the site of the cellars of the old Pince's School, demolished in 1898. The diagonal strip of new concrete on the right is the route of new underground telephone ducts connected with the arrival of STD in April 1966. Although busy there is ample space and not a foreign car in sight!

PETERSFIELD, *The Market Square 2004* P48702

Commanding this view is the brave 1982 Petersfield library trying to look like two buildings. The Square has had two refurbishments since 1965 and now features a tree in each corner. The cattle trough can be seen halfway up the left hand side of the photograph.

PETERSFIELD, *St Peter's Church 1898* 41317

The church appears as we know it today. Within the last 25 years it had undergone remodelling under the supervision of Sir Arthur Blomfield. In October 1950 the headstones were removed with the exception of that of John Small, a most famous early cricketer. This levelling helped the Urban District Council to maintain the closed churchyard in a decent state.

PETERSFIELD
St Peter's Church
2004 P48704

The church yard as it is today. The trees of 1898 had grown to over-maturity and been felled and the tombstones laid flat or used to clad the slopes that lead from the lower levels surrounding the church to the higher ones of the burial ground. The churchyard was closed for burials in 1856.

SHOPPING STREETS

IN THE 19TH CENTURY, Petersfield life revolved around its shops which until the latter part of the century were situated along the High Street and later (1885) included Chapel Street. The High Street was laid out to burgage plots from the town's inception and over the centuries these domestic plots saw their houses converted to trade use. Some provided the land for the inns for which the town grew famous. Samuel Pepys wrote 'Up early, and baited (ate) at Petersfield, in the room which the king lay in lately, at his being there.' Chapel Street, which had been the way out of town to Winchester, responded to the coming of the railway and the building of houses in Lavant Street with the mid-1880s construction of numerous retail premises. These remain much the same today.

PETERSFIELD
The High Street 1898 41319

These buildings excite interest. The famous Dolphin Inn built in the 1700s in the coaching days, was used by the military during World War I. In 1919 it became the County Secondary/High School for Girls. After that it was used as a temporary police station whilst the one in St Peter's Road received an early '60s revamp. Next door is the post office (1892) later to become a doctor's surgery. The adjoining house was well known as the dental surgery of Charlie Dickins but played its part in the history of Petersfield. Previously Tom Crawter installed batteries in the cellar and 'Clare Cross' became the first premises in Petersfield to have electric light.

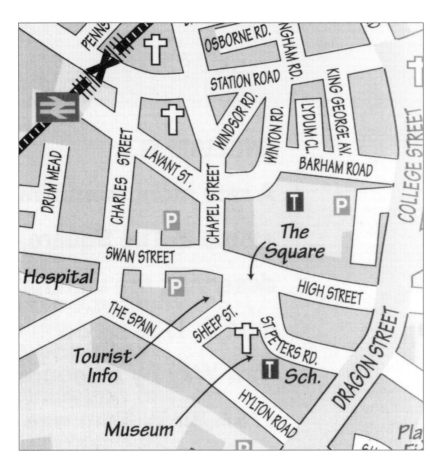

▶ **PETERSFIELD**
The High Street 2004
P48705

Compare this present-day picture with that of 1898; the first five buildings on the left, except one, have gone in order to make way for new developments in the sixties. The Cenotaph was erected in 1922 to a design inspired by the four blank panels on the Medici tombs (Michaelangelo) in Florence.

PETERSFIELD
The High Street
c1955 P48010

Grand Victorian banks are evident - the large white building towards the right-hand end looms over every other High Street building. On the other side of the road, by the Belisha beacon, is an earlier bank, its strong room is still in the basement. In the right foreground is the jewellery shop of Leo Williams and nearer to the camera the ground-coffee shop of E J Brewer.

PETERSFIELD
The High Street
2004 P48706

The High Street has just undergone a face-lift providing trees, allowing for limited car parking and a 20 mph speed limit. The Midland Bank, right at the end of the street, is now called HSBC.

▶ **PETERSFIELD**
The High Street c1955
P48042

The view is closed at the far end of the street by Norman Burton's, built in the early 1800s, and just to the right the café sign invites you to Frances Hill's tea rooms. The right of the picture shows Rowswell's sweets and tobacco shop and it is still there. The archway leads to Dog Alley, the scene of one of Flora Twort's lovely paintings, which used to go through to St Peter's Road. Beyond, E J Baker sold uncommonly good meat and the 'Punch and Judy', uncommonly good teas. On the left, Suter's was a quality shoe shop, later to become Kenney's; George Kenney was to enhance the shop's reputation still further.

◀ **PETERSFIELD**
The High Street 2004
P48707

E J Baker Ltd has given way to the chain store Superdrug. Rowswell's is still there and carrying on the same trade of paper, tobacco and sweets, but is now also an outlet for Lottery tickets. A sign of the times is that Cancer Research UK has taken over from Lynn the hairdresser.

▼ PETERSFIELD
The High Street c1965
P48076

Yet another evocative photograph from the past. Right is the Southdown booking office, with No. 9 the Square accommodating A G Suthers run by electrician 'Cherry' Messam. Just beyond Barclays Bank you can see the gates to Forrest Stores (also at Shere). They lead, via an apple-tree lined walk, to a small central car park - the large wooden gates providing the town with its notice board. This is where, in all weathers you would find Fred 'Benzo' Kimber selling the *Portsmouth Evening News*. One shop that must be mentioned is Lee Bros, Hairdressers, a discerning eye will see it behind the Players projecting sign in the middle

▲ **PETERSFIELD**
The High Street c1965
P48075

Top centre of the picture is No 1 the Square. A Tudor oak-framed building with knapped flint infill panels, its upper stories jetty over the ground floor; it is the oldest building in town. Above the ground floor of the shoe shop, John Farmer Ltd, can be seen a fire mark indicating the many years that the building has stood there.

▼ **PETERSFIELD**
The High Street 2004 P48708

Cubitt & West have changed their house style and it certainly is an improvement.
The old Forrest Stores building frontage gives the north side of the Square a
comfortable enduring appearance. Woolworths and Boots still snuggle side by side on
the left of this photograph.

▶ **PETERSFIELD**
The High Street c1965
P48078

Boot's is on the right, where
you could join their lending
library, and next to it
Woolworth's, where
immediately inside on the left
you used to be able to have a
'cuppa' and a bun. Further
along, that toddler on reins
celebrated her fortieth
birthday in early April 2004.
On the other side, G A Day Ltd
has superseded E J Baker, and
in turn has been replaced by
Superdrug. The little round
hanging sign indicates the
position of Rowswell's tobacco

and sweet shop; pop in there and look at the quality of the old wooden door. Pink's the Family Grocer gives testimony to
the the business empire of Alderman Pink of Portsmouth. For many years Cecil Carter managed Smeed's wine merchants.

◄ PETERSFIELD
Swan Street c1965
P48066

Do you see that canopy jutting over the pavement along the street? That was over the entrance to the Savoy cinema (1935), then showing what was described as a 'mildly funny' 1964 Inspector Clouseau film directed by Blake Edwards. The imposing building on the left side opposite the cinema is the offices of well-known solicitors Burley and Geach, the then senior partner was Leslie Burley. Southern Gas had replaced Davies the chemist, but G J Bassett, Ironmonger is just the same. The Centre Ring was previously the White Heather cafe but was to become John Dowler, Estate Agent, now Keats. By the way, Swan Street is named after the Swan Inn which once occupied the bank corner (National Provincial).

► PETERSFIELD
Chapel Street
c1955 P48040

The sun blinds on the right, next to George Bailey, Nurseryman, hide the identity of Whittingtons, Outfitters, soon to be Fosters. On the other side of the road, in a glimpse from the past, there are three sailors most probably from HMS Mercury at East Meon. The six-gabled building which is beyond them, sold for £12,000 in 1958.

PETERSFIELD, *Chapel Street c1955* P48012

That shop jutting out on the left is now Age of Elegance - as you enter look at the doorstep and you see, in mosaic, 'International Stores'. When this photograph was taken that's what it was. Just beyond the tanker, the shop was Timothy Whites. Coming towards us The Drum has an appearance which belies its age.

PETERSFIELD
Chapel Street
c1965 P48065

On the left The Glen Restaurant is now a notable kitchen shop, the Wool Shop next door became an outdoor clothing shop and Seals (Television) Ltd is but a hazy memory; it is now 'Petersfield Photographic'. New shops replace the side view looking along Chapel Street, ending in the gable end of the Petersfield Bookshop.

PETERSFIELD, *Chapel Street c1965* P48079

The 'Taylors' has been dropped from Timothy Whites; the shop was managed by Olive Pratt. The van appears to be delivering to furnishers Bowyer & Mendel and next door (No. 6) is the old Home & Colonial Stores. The chemist's opposite was W E Allen, later Moss's.

▶ **PETERSFIELD**
Lavant Street
1898 41322

This was a new street, built to exploit the coming of the railway - the station can be seen at the far end of the road. Many tobacconists kept the traditions of the shop on the left alive but it is now a restaurant. Those Victorian houses marching up the road have all succumbed to retail conversion. The gas streetlamp was one of the originals from 1862.

◀**PETERSFIELD**
Lavant Street 2004
P48710

What a difference a century makes! A line of genteel houses is now an indifferent row of shops. One early change was the construction of the large building halfway along on the right which is one of the town's two fish-and-chip shops. Prior to the '60s building there had been a well-known ironmongers and a dentist called Mr Must.

◄ **PETERSFIELD**
Lavant Street c1956
P48064

The station in the centre presides over this view. On the left D S Sole fulfilled decorators needs. Over the crossroads, with altered priority, are the offices of Jacobs & Hunt. The pitched roof to the tower has gone and street lighting shows an advance on the following picture (p. 60-61), here it is fluorescent!

PETERSFIELD
Lavant Street c1955
P48013

Only the names have changed. Austin's Library is now the Sue Ryder charity shop, Allsworth's ironmonger's, owned by Harry Hole, and immediately beyond, the Edwardian world of Martin & Triggs, Outfitters. Mortons were selling 'K' shoes and next door is now the home of One Tree Books. The suspended electric street light was one of Petersfield's first.

PETERSFIELD
Lavant Street 2004
P48711

The Railway Inn declined and was to make way for a development of retirement apartments. In their turn, the fluorescent streetlights have given way to high-pressure sodium luminaires. Jacobs & Hunt celebrated their centenary towards the end of the 20th century.

PETERSFIELD, *College Street 1898* 41323

College Street Public Hall (on the right) fell into disuse, became a motor-body repair shop and is now a car park. Next door, the Congregational, now United Reform church (1882), stands apparently unaltered, as does The Old College (1729) beyond. Opposite, note the chimney cowls at the premises of Gammon & Son, Decorators. This area was known as Stoneham Village.

PETERSFIELD
College Street 2004
P48712

The old Churcher's College became the offices of the Petersfield Rural District Council and now houses Hampshire County Council offices. The block of flats in the centre of the photo has replaced the motor business of Britnell and Crawter, indeed the flats are named Britnell House. The Good Intent on the left-hand side, sails on under the Whitbread flag.

PETERSFIELD, *College Street 1906* 54399

E J Baker, the High Street butcher, was delivering to the substantial houses, many of which still stand today. The large building on the left, at the far end of the street, was a Cheese Manufactory; during World War I it was one of many of the town's buildings that were pressed into service as barracks.

◀ **PETERSFIELD**
Sheep Street
1906 54400

Sheep Street, possibly Ship Street or Cheap Street, is shown here a hundred years ago, with most of the houses still intact today. Delightful Edwardian children's fashions are in evidence. This photograph must have been taken on a good day for room airing if the open windows are anything to go by.

◄ PETERSFIELD
College Street
2004 P48713

The cheese factory has made way for a motorcar sales room and workshop which has been replaced by high quality retirement homes. The cottage on the left is still there, having just completed a face-lift, but the shed construction which was the workshop of R Macklin, monumental mason, has made way for Barham Road which had been pushed through and developed by Mr Godfrey.

▲ **PETERSFIELD,** *Sheep Street c1965* P48058

If you need it, here is the evidence of unchanged houses over sixty years, although fish and chips are now on the national menu. The same original kerbstones are still in place at the time of writing. Look towards the bottom of the street and you see a glimpse of The Spain.

◄ PETERSFIELD
The Spain 1898
41326

The telephone pole, near the little girl, probably carried the wires for one of the town's first telephones from the nearby Cottage Hospital to the early telephone exchange above the High Street post office.

PETERSFIELD
The Spain 2004
P48714

Only the buttressed house remains of the interesting group in the 1898 photograph as the one on the left would now stand in the middle of a widened road. The other building has been replaced by three good examples of 20th-century design.

PETERSFIELD, *The Spain c1955* P48016

The same road widening seen in the previous picture led to the demolition of the white-painted end house in this shot. One would not now dream of walking down the centre of this road. The line of the paling on the left marked the boundary of the old Borough of Petersfield. Just behind the woman in white was an old borough boundary stone.

PETERSFIELD
The Spain 2004
P48715

The road widening has paid off and action by the inhabitants has secured the removal of unsightly overhead electricity distribution - well done! The new building in the background replaces the old Cottage Hospital with offices and apartments.

PETERSFIELD, *The Spain c1965* P48071

In the centre stands Hylton House, home of the last Lords of the Manor, later to become Seager House School, a girls' school evacuated from Hayling Island at the start of World War II, and then Moreton House school. More recently is was Churcher's Junior School.

▶ **PETERSFIELD**
The Cottage Hospital 1898
41333

Replaced by a new community hospital in April 1993, this lovely hospital was built in 1870 for £1,400. It was extended several times to accommodate further wards, day rooms, surgery room etc., but never lost its charm and homeliness. It had beautiful views over to the South Downs.

◀ **PETERSFIELD**
Station Road 1906
54401

Believe it or not, previously named Cow Legs Lane, this road was host to two Methodist Churches. The Primitive (1902) on the left, is now the Petersfield Masonic Lodge. The gentleman pushing his bicycle does not appear to be bothered by traffic and neither does the photographer.

▲ **PETERSFIELD,** *Station Road 2004* P48716

This photographer had to be up early one morning to take this comparable view. Gone are the metal railings which added some elegance to the properties; they were all swept away during World War II in the armaments drive. The imposing Methodist Church celebrated its centenary in 2003.

◀ **PETERSFIELD**
The Railway Restaurant and the Wesleyan Church 1906
54416

Edwardian style is now replacing the prim costumes of the Victorian years. The little house sandwiched between the church and the restaurant, was the home of Petersfield's well-known singer, Wilfred Brown. The Railway Restaurant gave way to Dolloway's (sweets & magazines) and then to Fields Antique Shop.

▼ **PETERSFIELD**
Methodist Church and the Corner Shop 2004 P48717

Fields Antique Shop passed into memory in the early '80s and a new retailing form took its place - the Eight until Late shop, this being its latest incarnation. Out of sight, recent extensions to the church have created a worthwhile centre on which to focus its activities.

▶ **PETERSFIELD**
Station Road 1898
41320

This is the junction of Chapel Street with a now widened Tilmore Road. The cottage on the left still exists, although now substantially altered. The sign by the people on the footpath advertises Woods, Coal & Coke Merchants, later to become 'Punch' Mullard's builder's yard and presently, Spinningfield House flats.

PETERSFIELD
Station Road 2004
P48718

The cottage on the left has been given a new lease of life judging by its appearance. For those with long memories it was at one time the offices of Frank Stubbs, Estate Agents. On the right there is a dwelling from the early '20s but the garage at the side of the road was there in the original photograph.

▶ **PETERSFIELD**
Dragon Street c1965
P48046

The road to the seaside. Basil Mould, the builder, had made his mark on the town with the Pulens Lane develoment. Again on the right, underneath the AA sign, Hall, Pain and Foster were advertising Wadhams 'Valuable Freehold Premises' for sale. This sale helped Wadham - Stringer to construct a large showroom/workshop development in College Street. The car showroom shown is now an art gallery. Opposite,

the imposing three-storey Dragon House (set back slightly from the road) is home to a dentist's surgery. The Toby Jug next door then accommodated Henry Court, Boot and Shoe Repairer, in a soon to be demolished left-hand wing.

PETERSFIELD
The Red Lion Hotel
1906 54417

The advent of the motor carriage did not prevent the hotel advertising the stables at the back of this famous coaching hotel. The Automobile Club monogram hanging under the hotel sign had obviously appealed to the two car owners and most probably the owner of the early motorcycle. The view is unchanged today.

PETERSFIELD
The Red Lion Hotel
2004 P48719

Instantly recognisable as the Red Lion of 1906, it is now a Beefeater restaurant and pub. The upstairs public hall in which dances, public meetings and film society gatherings used to be held, has been converted to accommodation. Note the sign directing cars to the Festival Hall (1935), host to so much of the town's activity.

PETERSFIELD, *The Lake c1955* P48035

Known in Petersfield as 'the Pond' and created out of three very boggy areas in 1732, this spot has never ceased to attract visitors from miles around. A very similar photograph could easily be taken now, fifty years later.

PETERSFIELD
The Lake c1955
P48029

Victorian taste dictated that large conifers should be planted everywhere and The Heath Pond was no exception. In some cases now overmature, they have been features of the landscape for all living memory.

PETERSFIELD, *The Heath Pond 2004* P48720

After 50 years, very much as one would expect, with the exception that one of the pine trees has been removed. In the intervening years the bank has been revetted against erosion, and the millenium celebrated by the natural path for wheel chairs that encircles the pond.

SHEET AND STEEP

THESE similar sounding villages have totally different characters, with Sheet being a close-knit community and Steep being spread over a large area. Sheet virtually touches the town and snuggles around its village hall on The Green. The road to London passed along what is now Village Street, up Town Lane and to Portsmouth via Petersfield. The establishment of the Sheet to Cosham Turnpike (1721) led to the Sheet bypass being built from the bottom of Adhurst Hill to the roundabout at the top of Shear Hill. The village enjoys an engaging social life with the Queen's Head and the adjacent village hall as the focus.

Steep is a widespread parish which stretches out to Steep Marsh and even beyond Sheet to the border of Sussex. Not so much a village but at its heart it has Church Road with the Memorial Hall, the ancient church, the school, Bedales School and Restalls, a private house which is thought to date back to the reign of Henry VII. What it does have is a formidable list of well-known 20th-century personages with connections to the village - Edward Barnsley (furniture maker), Edward Thomas (poet) and Sir Alec Guinness (actor) to name but a few.

SHEET, *Village Green 1898* 41344

Its brand new village hall, right of centre, is outwardly much the same today although the inside is much changed. The Sir Arthur Blomfield church, dedicated to St Mary Magdalen, was built a generation before, almost at the same time as the school nestling behind the trees on the left. The carts brought provisions every day from Petersfield.

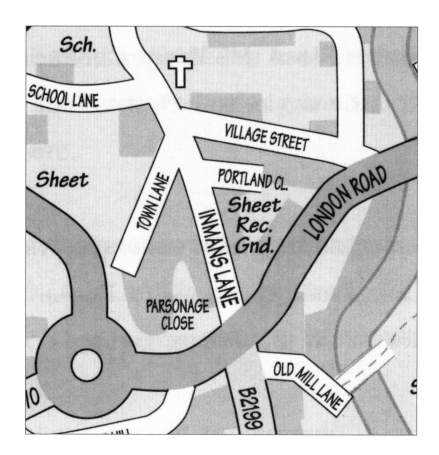

▶ **SHEET**
*The Church and
Green 1898*
41345

St Mary's, with an
open green in front,.
although in the
middle is a young
horse chestnut, the
replacement for the
one planted in 1887
which died. This
beautiful tree is now
the pride of the
village; it was
planted to celebrate
the 1897 diamond
jubilee of Her
Majesty Queen
Victoria.

◀ **SHEET**
The Green 1898
41346

The about-turn view of the last picture, this shows the unmistakable path beaten across The Green to the Queen's Head. Between the village hall and the large windowless barn on the left, the picturesque group of houses has now been converted to Lion House. Village Street leads away downhill to the old post office.

▶ **SHEET**
The Post Office 1898 41348

This interesting picture shows the bridge over the Rother at the bottom of Adhurst Hill. The post office on the right superseded the toll house on the turnpike (1711). Note the semicircular door made to reflect the similar shape of the toll keeper's office. The old convalescent home in the background is now two houses.

► **SHEET,** *The Post Office Door 2004* S107701

The site of the post office is now flattened ground with nothing to show, but its semicircular door lives on as the front door to a house, not a mile away from its original position. Built like a stable door, it enabled the turnpike toll keeper to reach out and take his dues while staying out of the weather.

▼ **SHEET,** *Sandy Lane 1898* 41353

Ruts either side of this ravine prove the use of this short cut to West Mark. Then a shady summer drive, now this cleft in the sandstone is overgrown and impassable - all part of the Sheet Common adventure.

► **SHEET**
A View on the Rother 1898
41350

Here the downstream mill pond was backing up the river level where young lads used to swim in summer. Old Sheet Mill is in the background, ushering the Rother on its way past Pulborough and Arundel on the way to the sea at Littlehampton.

◄ **SHEET**
*The Mill and an
Old Cottage 1898*
41351

In this photograph
the line of washing on
the right seems to
indicate a Monday
morning. A loaded
cart has been backed
up, with its load of
corn for milling, and
the millpond looks to
be in good order. The
trap behind, with
bowler-hatted driver,
belonged to C Evans.

▶ **STEEP**
*Kettlebrook
1898* 41362

In this photograph the cottages had only recently had their thatch replaced and the wall, next to the woman with the dog, rebuilt. The stream and its bridge are a favourite 'Pooh Sticks' venue for the many children who play here.

◀**STEEP**
Kettlebrook 2004
S188701

Here is a view that never changes, as witnessed by this present-day photograph. Now there are railings alongside the path next to Kettlebrook. Follow this path and you are on the old road to Liss.

▲ **STEEP,** *All Saints' Church 1898* 41358

An open view of the 12th-century church from across Church Road, with neither hedges nor yew trees. Just out of the picture is the lych gate built in 1893, replacing one that had collapsed under the weight of snow in a previous April!

◄ **STEEP**
An Old Cottage 1898 41363

Described by Edward Thomas the poet, as 'hunching soft' in Lutcombe Bottom, this idyllic scene below Stoner was lost to us in the late forties with the demolition of the cottage. Called Keeper's Cottage, it serves to remind us of an age gone by.

WEST MEON AND HARTING

THESE VILLAGES are to the east and west of Petersfield. Harting is the larger and has an uncanny knack of cropping up in conversation all over the country as a favourite place to call 'home'. Like Buriton, it shelters close under the protection of the South Downs which gives a clue to its origins. H G Wells spent his formative years here living at Uppark. Due to the invention of the hydraulic ram, Uppark was one of the first great houses to be built at the top of a hill.

Harting is a much sought-after village in which to live.

West Meon was in all probability a village born of the trade in fleeces; it can be found on the road that connects Fareham and Gosport to London. A little village that has managed to keep its shop and its post office, it is famed for the huge display of snowdrops during January and February around the church just to the south of the village.

◀ **WEST MEON**
The Viaduct
c1955 W488012

This long-gone railway (1903 - February 1955) and its demolished viaduct, played an important part in the preparations for D Day, bringing material and troops to their embarkation points. Just look at the telephone pole with four eight-way arms and a 'cow horn' on top.

WEST MEON
High Street
c1965 W488031

In common with many villages, the local garage, Meon Motors, has gone and is commemorated by 'Ye Olde Garage House' built on the site. The Thomas Lord pub acknowledges the debt owed by English cricket to the West Meon founder of Lord's cricket ground.

WEST MEON, *The Village and Church c1965* W488038

It is heartening to think that this view has changed only in the growth of the background trees over 40 years and the removal of thatch from one of the 18th-century cottages. See how they exist in harmony with their Victorian successors.

▼ **WEST MEON,** *The Village and Church 2004* W488701

The flagpole still stands guard over the War Memorial and the flag is flown on appropriate occasions. The thatch has been removed from one of the cottages and the little wicket gate next to the road has been removed for safety reasons. You can still see the line of the gate in the brickwork.

▶ **HARTING**
The Church and the Village 1906 54413

Familiar to many, the church nestles in the shelter of the South Downs. Large horse chestnuts now break the roof line but the cottages still lie tranquil within the church's reach. H G Wells walked from Portsmouth to Harting to meet his mother coming from this church.

◀ **SOUTH HARTING**
The Square c1955
S827004

Is the woman in the top window cleaning it or simply determined to be in the photograph? The one-time butcher's shop was, at the time of this photograph, an antiques shop. It would have been known to H G Wells when he was a boy at the nearby stately home, Uppark.

▶ On the stall riser in the picture above, the curious will see the head of a magnificent bull. This gives a clue to the former use of the premises as a butcher's shop. Those days have long been gone but not forgotten by Harting's oldest veterans.

SOUTH HARTING
The Ship Inn 1906
54415

E J Beach, Proprietor, boldly announces the board above the pony and trap, apparently hired for a drive during one of those Edwardian summers that never seemed to end. Mr Beach advertised 'good accommodation for cyclists, catering for parties, and good stabling'.

EAST HARTING, *The Village 1906* 54414

Rose growers in these villages must have benefitted from passing horses if the state of this road is anything to go by! This is all part of the country life that has surrounded Petersfield for centuries; may it always be so.

INDEX

Buriton 14-15, 16, 17

East Harting 88

East Meon 18-19, 20-21, 22-23

Froxfield Green 24-25, 26, 27,

Harting 86

The Lake 74, 75

Liss 28-29, 30, 31, 32, 33, 34-35

Red Lion Hotel 73, 74

Sheet 76-77, 78-79, 80-81

The Spain 65, 66, 67

South Harting 86-87, 88

Steep 82-83

West Liss 30-31

West Meon 84-85, 86

PETERSFIELD

Chapel Street 55, 56, 57

College Street 62, 63, 64-65

Cottage Hospital 68-69

Dragon Street 71

From Tilmore 36-37

High Street 46-47, 48-49, 50-51, 52-53, 54

Lavant Street 58-59, 60-61, 62

Market Place 38-39, 40-41, 42, 43, 44

St Peter's Church 45

Railway Restaurant 69

Sheep Street 64, 65

Station Road 68, 70

Swan Street 54-55,

Heath Pond 75

Wesleyan Church 70

NAMES OF SUBSCRIBERS

The following people have kindly supported this book by subscribing to copies before publication

Joyce & David Allen

Doreen Beesly, Petersfield

Michel & Sylvie Bentot, Maire du Barentin

Olive Boniface

Miss Laura J Bristol, South Harting

In Memory of Richard & Ellen Bunce, Petersfield

To Four Generations of the Burley Family

Andrew Chown, Petersfield

Vaughan Clarke, Petersfield

Dorothy & Tom Collard, Palmers Farm

Janet Crockford

Jackie Curtis, Liss Forest

To Dad all our love Jane & Clive

Eddie Dawes and Family

Mr & Mrs S Dunning, Chichester

Brian & Audrey Dutton, Petersfield

Julian Edwards

The Elsey Family, Petersfield

Peter George Fisher, Sheep St, Petersfield

Norman Stanley Flatt, Clanfield

In Memory of the Gander Family, trading from 1800's - 1950's

Mr R A & Mrs J P Gard, Petersfield

E D & J Hampton

Jill, Marc & Nicola Haynes of Petersfield, 2004

John & Morag Hewens of Petersfield, 2004

Jacqueline Hick & Peter Garratt

Edna & Joyce Hick

The Holloway Family, Petersfield

Mr & Mrs C Jacobs, Petersfield

Miss H Jacobs, Southampton

Happy Birthday Les Jarman 18th July 2004

David Jeffery

Mr & Mrs Peter Jones

Jane & Bob Jones, Locks Heath

Roy Kersley

Susie & Philip Lacey

Mr & Mrs R Lacey

Mr C R Lacey

H. Lee & Son, Hairdresser, The Square

With love to Pollyanna Lowery, 2004

Paul Martin

Mr David Matthews

Barham Rd remembered,
    Paul & June Molloy

Mr & Mrs M J L Mordle, Petersfield

The Nicholson Family

Tom Norgate

Linda, David, James & Matthew Papworth

Tim & Olivia Passingham

Brian & Judith Peake, Petersfield

Josy & John Petley-Jones, Liss Forest

Tony & Beryl Peyton-Bruhl

Katie Pitt

Pour Rémi Plaud, Au-Delà des Mers

G V Ralph, Portsmouth

George Rankine, Petersfield

The Rogers Family

To our friends at the Rotary Club of
    Emmeloord

Rotary Emmeloord

To our friends at the Rotary Club of Thurles

Mr J Scarr

J & D Seaward

Terry Shorten

John & Carol Stabb, Petersfield

Col Julian Starmer-Smith, O B E

Mr R E & Mrs M H Stokes, Buriton

Guido e Louisa Stuani

The Vincent Family, Petersfield

In Memory of Vera & Harry Walker

Pam & Howard Walsh

The Watkinson Family

Roger & Pat Wettone

To Dad, Brian Whitehouse, 'Happy
    Memories'

John & Paula Wigley, Petersfield

Pam & Don Wilding, Steep

Derek T D Williams, O B E

John Wood, Petersfield

Sue Wright, Langrish

Philip & Penny Young, Petersfield

FRITH PRODUCTS & SERVICES

Francis Frith would doubtless be pleased to know that the pioneering publishing venture he started in 1860 still continues today. Over a hundred and forty years later, The Francis Frith Collection continues in the same innovative tradition and is now one of the foremost publishers of vintage photographs in the world. Some of the current activities include:

Interior Decoration

Today Frith's photographs can be seen framed and as giant wall murals in thousands of pubs, restaurants, hotels, banks, retail stores and other public buildings throughout the country. In every case they enhance the unique local atmosphere of the places they depict and provide reminders of gentler days in an increasingly busy and frenetic world.

Product Promotions

Frith products are used by many major companies to promote the sales of their own products or to reinforce their own history and heritage. Frith promotions have been used by Hovis bread, Courage beers, Scots Porage Oats, Colman's mustard, Cadbury's foods, Mellow Birds coffee, Dunhill pipe tobacco, Guinness, and Bulmer's Cider.

Genealogy and Family History

As the interest in family history and roots grows world-wide, more and more people are turning to Frith's photographs of Great Britain for images of the towns, villages and streets where their ancestors lived; and, of course, photographs of the churches and chapels where their ancestors were christened, married and buried are an essential part of every genealogy tree and family album.

Frith Products

All Frith photographs are available Framed or just as Mounted Prints and Posters (size 23 x 16 inches). These may be ordered from the address below. From time to time other products - Address Books, Calendars, Table Mats, etc - are available.

The Internet

Already fifty thousand Frith photographs can be viewed and purchased on the internet through the Frith websites and a myriad of partner sites.

For more detailed information on Frith companies and products, look at these sites:

www.francisfrith.co.uk
www.francisfrith.com
(for North American visitors)

See the complete list of Frith Books at:

www.francisfrith.co.uk

This web site is regularly updated with the latest list of publications from the Frith Book Company. If you wish to buy books relating to another part of the country that your local bookshop does not stock, you may purchase on-line.

For further information, trade, or author enquiries please contact us at the address below:
The Francis Frith Collection, Frith's Barn, Teffont, Salisbury, Wiltshire, England SP3 5QP.
Tel: +44 (0)1722 716 376 Fax: +44 (0)1722 716 881   Email: sales@francisfrith.co.uk

See Frith books on the internet at www.francisfrith.co.uk

FREE MOUNTED PRINT

Mounted Print
Overall size 14 x 11 inches

Fill in and cut out this voucher and return
it with your remittance for £2.25 (to cover postage and handling). Offer valid for delivery to UK addresses only.

Choose any photograph included in this book.
Your SEPIA print will be A4 in size. It will be mounted in a cream mount with a burgundy rule line (overall size 14 x 11 inches).

Order additional Mounted Prints at HALF PRICE (only £7.49 each*)
If you would like to order more Frith prints from this book, possibly as gifts for friends and family, you can buy them at half price (with no additional postage and handling costs).

Have your Mounted Prints framed
For an extra £14.95 per print* you can have your mounted print(s) framed in an elegant polished wood and gilt moulding, overall size 16 x 13 inches (no additional postage and handling required).

---

* IMPORTANT!

These special prices are only available if you order at the same time as you order your free mounted print. You must use the ORIGINAL VOUCHER on this page (no copies permitted). We can only despatch to one address.

Send completed Voucher form to:
The Francis Frith Collection, Frith's Barn, Teffont, Salisbury, Wiltshire SP3 5QP

Voucher
*for **FREE** and Reduced Price Frith Prints*

Please do not photocopy this voucher. Only the original is valid, so please fill it in, cut it out and return it to us with your order.

Picture ref no	Page no	Qty	Mounted @ £7.49	Framed + £14.95	Total Cost
		1	Free of charge*	£	£
			£7.49	£	£
			£7.49	£	£
			£7.49	£	£
			£7.49	£	£
			£7.49	£	£
Please allow 28 days for delivery			* Post & handling (UK)		£2.25
			Total Order Cost		£

Title of this book . . . .

I enclose a cheque/postal order for £ . . . .
made payable to 'The Francis Frith Collection'

OR please debit my Mastercard / Visa / Switch / Amex card
(credit cards please on all overseas orders), details below

Card Number

Issue No (Switch only)   Valid from (Amex/Switch)

Expires   Signature

Name Mr/Mrs/Ms . . . .

Address . . . .

. . . .

. . . .

. . . . Postcode . . . .

Daytime Tel No . . . .

Email . . . .

Valid to 31/12/05

Free Print – see overleaf

Would you like to find out more about Francis Frith?

We have recently recruited some entertaining speakers who are happy to visit local groups, clubs and societies to give an illustrated talk documenting Frith's travels and photographs. If you are a member of such a group and are interested in hosting a presentation, we would love to hear from you.

Our speakers bring with them a small selection of our local town and county books, together with sample prints. They are happy to take orders. A small proportion of the order value is donated to the group who have hosted the presentation. The talks are therefore an excellent way of fundraising for small groups and societies.

Can you help us with information about any of the Frith photographs in this book?

We are gradually compiling an historical record for each of the photographs in the Frith archive. It is always fascinating to find out the names of the people shown in the pictures, as well as insights into the shops, buildings and other features depicted.

If you recognize anyone in the photographs in this book, or if you have information not already included in the author's caption, do let us know. We would love to hear from you, and will try to publish it in future books or articles.

Our production team

Frith books are produced by a small dedicated team at offices in the converted Grade II listed 18th-century barn at Teffont near Salisbury, illustrated above. Most have worked with the Frith Collection for many years. All have in common one quality: they have a passion for the Frith Collection. The team is constantly expanding, but currently includes:

Paul Baron, Jason Buck, John Buck, Ruth Butler, Heather Crisp, David Davies, Isobel Hall, Julian Hight, Peter Horne, James Kinnear, Karen Kinnear, Tina Leary, Stuart Login, David Marsh, Sue Molloy, Glenda Morgan, Wayne Morgan, Kate Rotondetto, Dean Scource, Eliza Sackett, Terence Sackett, Sandra Sampson, Adrian Sanders, Sandra Sanger, Julia Skinner, Lewis Taylor, Shelley Tolcher, Lorraine Tuck and Jeremy Walker.